I0697913

TABLE OF CONTENTS

DEDICATION

To my mother Linda Canady,

I hope you are proud of me today and always. I want to apologize for any trouble I caused you when I was younger, and for making your parenting skills look bad. But know that I have learned from my mistakes, and I am a better person today because of your love and guidance.

To my brother Angelo "LO GOTTI," thank you for always helping me find the truth, even when it's hard to face. Your business, "ASAP," is something to be proud of, and I am proud of you.

To my sister Antownna, thank you for taking in my children in my time of need. You have always had my back and held our family together. I am grateful for your unwavering support and love.

To my father Anthony, thank you for never hiding the darkness of the streets and keeping it real with me. You taught me to never be afraid and to be strong, and for that, I am forever grateful.

To my best friend Nikki, I can see a good life for you and your child. Keep striving for greatness, and I am always here to support you.

To my bonus brother Payton, together we are dangerously strong. You call me the THOUGHT, and yourself the EXECUTOR, and I believe it's true. Let's continue to make waves and make a difference.

To my woman Bee, thank you for inspiring me every day. I wish you the best in all your endeavors, and I am always here to support you.

And finally, to my children, I will teach you everything I know if you are willing to listen. You are the future, and it's important to me that I lead the way to a better tomorrow.

To my cousins and friends I just want to let you know that I'm always here for you whenever you need me. Whether you're going through a tough time or just need someone to talk to, I'm here to listen and support you in any way I can. You all mean the world to me, and I cherish the time we spend together. I may not always remember everyone's name to shout out, but I want you to know that I love and appreciate each and every one of you. Let's keep PUSHing

As Maya Angelou said, "I've learned that people will forget what you said, people will forget what you did, but people will never forget how you made them feel." I hope that I can make all of you feel proud, loved, and supported.

As Frederick Douglass said, "It is easier to build strong children than to repair broken men." I am committed to building strong children and making a positive impact in their lives.

And as Angela Davis said, "I am no longer accepting the things I cannot change. I am changing the things I cannot accept." I will continue to work towards a better tomorrow, and I hope to inspire all of you to do the same.

With love and gratitude, keep it pushing,

Anton Canady

SUCCESS AHEAD

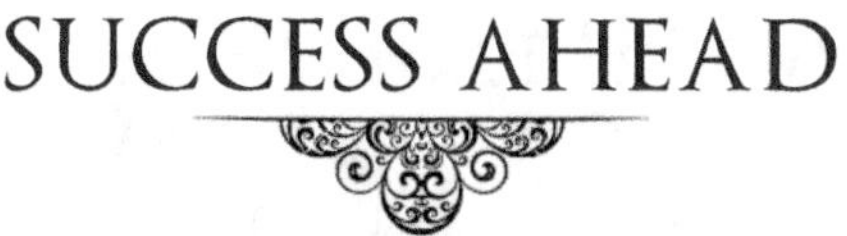

There's a road ahead, so bright and clear,
A path to success, so very near,
Yet sometimes we stumble, sometimes we fall,
And find ourselves stuck, with no hope at all.

But don't give up, don't lose your way,
For success is waiting, day by day,
You have the power, you have the will,
To climb that mountain, and reach the hill.

Take a step forward, and then another,
With each small victory, you'll discover,
That you have the strength, the courage, the heart,
To overcome any obstacle, right from the start.

So don't be afraid, don't be dismayed,
Your dreams are waiting, they won't fade,
Just keep on pushing, keep on trying,
And soon enough, you'll see success flying.

For you have what it takes, within your soul,
To achieve anything, and take control,
So embrace the challenge, and never sway,
For success is yours, in every way.

FATHER'S DREAM

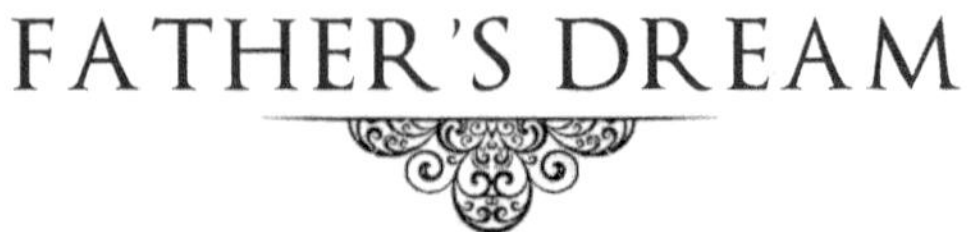

A father, a hero, strong and true,
His family's rock, in all they do,
Through hard times and struggles,
He stood tall, working late into the night,
To give them his all.

His eyes heavy with tiredness,
et still he persists, for his love for his family, never desists,
He knows the sacrifice, he knows the pain, but he does it
all, for their gain.

He labors long hours, in sweat and toil, for he knows that
his family's happiness is his spoil, he never complains, he
never falters, for his family's future, he's the sole alter.

His love knows no bounds, his strength never wavers,
he's their shield, their protector, in every danger, he holds
them close, and wipes away their tears, and gives them
strength, to face their fears.

And though the night may be long, and the road rough,
He walks with them, and never enough,
For his love is eternal, and his sacrifice supreme, a father's
love, the ultimate dream.

THE BEE AND THE GORILLA

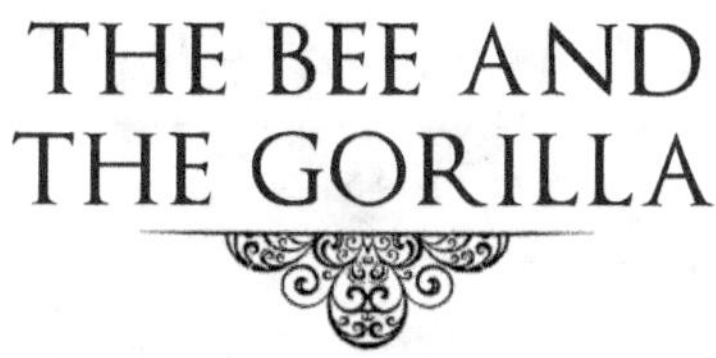

A bee and a gorilla, an unlikely pair,
Set out on a journey, without a care.
They faced the wilderness, the wild and rough,
Together they went, through mountains and gruff.

The bee flew ahead, scouting for danger,
While the gorilla lumbered on, a gentle ranger.
They shared the road, each one in its own way,
And through the thickets, they made their way.

The bee buzzed happily, leading the way,
Showing the gorilla, where to step and sway.
The gorilla listened, with a keen ear,
And followed the bee, without any fear.

They traveled for days, through heat and cold,
The bee and gorilla, a tale to be told.
They braved the wild, without any dread,
And stayed together, till the journey's end.

The bee and gorilla, a bond unbreakable,
A friendship formed, unshakable and remarkable.
They proved to all, that even the unlikeliest pair,
Can journey together, without a single care.

CLAP 4 EM

I see them rise, to claim their prize,
A triumph earned, through endless tries,
And though it's not me, who takes the stage,
I feel the joy, the hope, the rage.

For I know the struggle, the pain, the fear,
The countless hours, the shedded tear,
That it takes to reach, the top of the game,
To win at life, and never be the same.

So when I see, someone else succeed,
My heart is full, and I take the lead,
To cheer them on, to shout their name,
And celebrate, their moment of fame.

For their success, is a victory for us all,
A beacon of hope, that we can stand tall,
And achieve our dreams, no matter how far,
For they never gave up, and we can be like a star.

So let us rejoice, in the triumphs we see,
And use their strength, to inspire you and me,
For with each victory, we build the fire,
To reach new heights, and never tire.

And though we may stumble, and fall to the ground,
We know that victory, can always be found,
If we keep pushing, and never give in,
For we too can win, and let the glory begin.

SIT ON WINGS

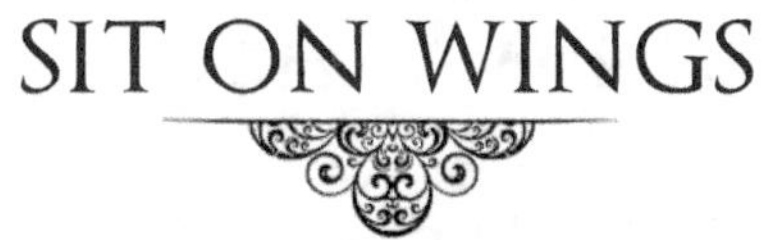

Women, do not give up on a man,
For they too, need love from a woman's hand,
But do not let them sit on your wings,
Or bring you down, with their selfish things.

You are a queen, a force to be reckoned with,
And your worth is not tied, to any man's myth,
You have a heart, that is pure and true,
And you deserve a love, that is equally due.

But beware, of the men who take and take,
And leave you empty, with a heart that aches,
They will try to clip your wings, and hold you down,
But you are not a prize, to be won or found.

So love them, but do not lose yourself,
For your heart is your wealth, your truest wealth,
And when you stand strong, and know your worth,
You will attract a love, that is meant for rebirth.

For a man who truly loves you, will lift you higher,
And support your dreams, and your burning fire,
He will not hold you back, or weigh you down,
But rather, he will walk beside you, with a love profound.

So do not give up, on a man who deserves your love,
But do not sacrifice yourself, for someone above,
For you are a woman, a queen in your right,
And you deserve a love, that is pure and bright.

ME VS THEM

Amidst the chaos of this world so loud,
 stand alone, my heart my shroud,
For nobody understands the depth of my soul,
And the challenges that make me whole.

But I am learning to appreciate myself,
To find my worth, my own inner wealth,
For in this journey, I am not alone,
And I can make this world my home.

I do not care for the opinions of the crowd,
If they are not positive, they are not allowed,
For I have learned to listen to my own voice,
And to make my own life, my own choice.

For I am unique, a precious gem,
And my light shines bright, like a diadem,
And though the world may not see my worth,
I know my value, and it is of great girth.

So I stand tall, amidst the noise and fray,
And I will keep moving forward, day by day,
For I am learning to appreciate myself,
And to find my happiness, my own true wealth.

WHY MONEY?

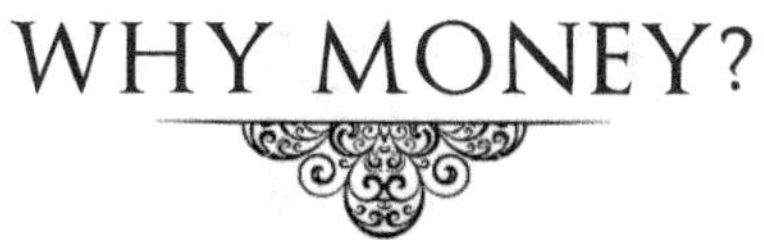

Money, a tool, a means to an end,
A necessity, for choices to extend,
But do we value it, more than we should?
Or do we use it, for our own good?

For money, alone, is not the key,
To happiness, or prosperity,
But it can open doors, and provide,
Options, for choices we want to decide.

It's not about the wealth, or the fame,
But the freedom, to play life's game,
To pursue our dreams, and our goals,
And to live life, as a whole.

Money, a means, to create our way,
To open doors, and seize the day,
For it gives us options, and the power,
To live life, to the fullest, every hour.

So let us use it, with wisdom and care,
For it can bring joy, or despair,
But with the right mindset, and the right intent,
Money can be a tool, for a life well spent.

1 MONTH 2 EARS

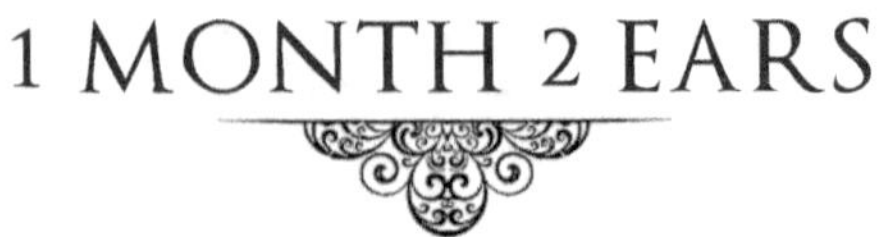

Two ears to hear, and one mouth to speak,
A lesson in life, so simple, yet unique,
For in this balance, we find harmony,
And learn the art, of true empathy.

With two ears to listen, we gain insight,
Into others' worlds, their pain and plight,
And through this empathy, we can connect,
And show our love, with respect.

For when we speak, we must choose our words,
And listen first, before they are heard,
For it is through understanding, we can grow,
And in our hearts, true wisdom will flow.

So let us listen more, and speak less,
And in this balance, we'll find success,
For in this world, with all its strife,
The power of listening, can change a life.

SLEEP 4 MILLENARIES

Sleep is for millionaires, they say,
The ones who've made it, in their own way,
For they've worked hard, and sacrificed,
And now they sleep, with peace and pride.

But what of us, who've yet to climb,
The ladder of success, in our time?
Do we work hard, with all our might,
Until we sleep, in the still of the night?

For sleep is not a luxury, but a need,
To rest and recharge, our bodies and creed,
But to achieve our goals, we must push,
And work tirelessly, until we have enough.

Sleep is for millionaires, it's true,
But it's not just for them, it's for me and you,
For we can work hard, and still find time,
To rest and recover, to reach our prime.

So let us work hard, with all our might,
But never forget, to rest at night,
For in this balance, we'll find success,
And in our dreams, we'll find happiness

MY CHOICE

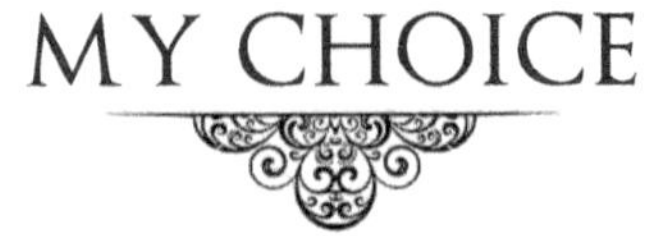

People see me and they think they know,
They see my strength and assume
I'll throw My weight around, and cause a scene,
But that's not who I want to be seen.

They don't know that I could destroy,
And leave chaos in my employ,
But instead I choose a different path,
And practice non-violence with all my craft.

For me, the worst type of violence,
Is the kind that causes silence,
The kind that brings destruction and pain,
And leaves nothing but regret and disdain.

So, I'll choose to use my strength and might,
To stand up for what I know is right,
And fight for justice, love, and peace,
Until all hatred and violence cease.

For even though I may seem strong,
It's in non-violence that I truly belong,
And by choosing to take this path,
I hope to inspire a better aftermath.

So let the world see me and judge,
But they'll never know the truest grudge,
Is the one that's left to fester and rot,
When violence is chosen over love and thought.

SUNDAY ALWAYS COMES

Sunday always comes, to wash away the stress and strife,
A day to find our strength above,
And seek the word of God in life.

As we enter the House of Hope,
Our hearts are filled with peace and grace,
the burdens of the week are gone,
And we feel love's sweet embrace.

The words of truth and hope we hear,
Inspire us to be our best,
To love each other, conquer fear,
And rise above life's constant test.

Sunday always comes,
To remind us of what's true and right,
A day to leave our worries clear,
And bask in love's eternal light.

In the House of Hope, we'll find our way,
And lift our spirits high and bright,
For Sunday always comes to stay,
And fill our hearts with pure delight.
Sunday always comes

FEELS LIKE FIRE

From the ghetto streets,
I rose up high, Where the struggle and the pain never
seem to die, But I had a vision burning in my heart,
And a determination to make a new start.

I may not be where I want to be,
But I'm not where I used to be,
I fought and I clawed my way through,
And now success is mine, it's true.

I saw a way out of this cycle of poverty,
And I took it, despite the naysayers' mockery,
I knew that if I could just keep my focus,
I could rise above the chaos and the locus.

I partied and had fun along the way,
But always kept my goals in sight each day,
I worked hard and never lost my sight,
And now I'm soaring high like a kite.

From the bottom to the top I climbed,
And every step was a victory I find,
I refused to let my circumstances hold me back,
And now success is mine, no turning back.

So to all my brothers and sisters in the struggle,
Keep fighting, don't ever let your dreams crumble,
If you see a vision, take it with all your might,
And you too can rise above the blight.

It may not be easy, but it's worth the fight,
To break the cycle and soar to new heights,
So keep your head up, and your eyes on the prize,
And success will be yours, as sure as the skies.

POWER BEHIND MONEY

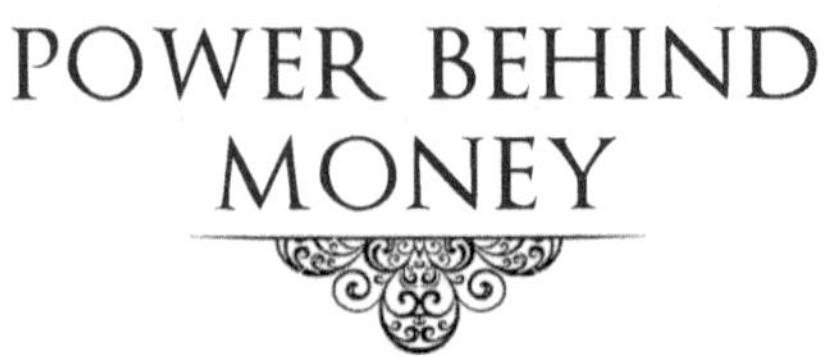

Money has a power that's hard to ignore,
It can open doors, and so much more,
It can bring you pleasure, and ease your pain,
But the power it holds, can also be a bane.

On one side, money can do good,
It can feed the hungry, and help the needy stood,
It can create opportunities, and give us hope,
And with it, we can live life, and freely elope.

On the other side, money can do harm,
It can create greed, and lead to an alarm,
It can cause division, and break families apart,
And with it, we can lose ourselves, and our heart.

It's easy to get caught up in the power of wealth,
To measure our worth by what's in our bankshelf,
But we must remember, that money is fleeting,
And in the end, it's not what we'll be needing.

For when our time comes, and we face our fate,
Money won't matter, it will be too late,
We'll be thinking of love, and the moments we've shared,
Of the people we've touched, and the lives we've repaired.

So let us enjoy life, but not waste it on wealth,
Let us find joy in moments, and good health,

Let us make memories, and leave a legacy behind,
For that's where true power lies, in the heart and mind.

HE TRIED

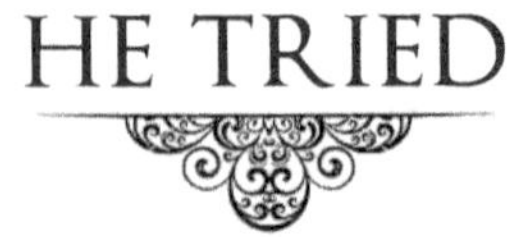

She hated him, this man who tried to help,
With all her heart, she wished he'd go away,
She couldn't see the kindness in his help,
Blinded by anger, she couldn't sway.

He tried his best to make her see,
To help her out of the darkness and the pain,
But she just couldn't let it be,
Her hate for him, a never ending chain.

He wondered what he could have done,
To make her hate him so very much,
He wished to show her that he cared,
And to heal the wounds of her broken touch.

But there was nothing he could do,
To change the way she felt inside,
So he moved forward with his life,
And left her hate behind.

He knew that someday she would see,
The kindness that he tried to give,
And he would be there with open arms,
For her to finally forgive.

For in his heart, he knew the truth,
That he had done all that he could do,
And if she never saw his worth,
His love would still ring true.

WHO ARE YOU

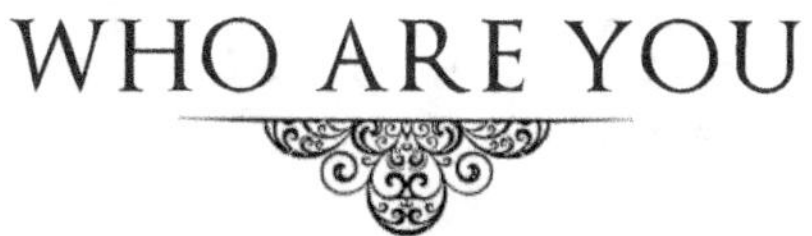

It's not what you are, but who you are,
That defines you in this world afar,
For in your heart lies your true worth,
Beyond the things that mark your birth.

Your race, your gender, your class, your creed,
May shape the way that others perceive,
But deep inside, where it counts the most,
Is where your true identity boasts.

For it's your character that stands the test,
Of time and all that comes abreast,
The way you treat your fellow man,
And the deeds you do with your own hand.

Your heart is what makes you who you are, Not the
things that may set you apart,
For in the end, it's love that wins,
And the light within that forever glints.

So hold your head up high, my friend,
And know that you are more than just a trend,
For in your soul lies all that's true,
And the world is blessed to have you.

TAKING STEPS

Through the wilderness I roam,
A journey of change, a journey of home,
For deep within my soul,
I know, I must transform, I must grow.

The road ahead is tough and steep,
With obstacles I must learn to leap,
But with each step, I shed my fears,
And gain the strength to persevere.

I leave behind the person I was,
And embrace a new, stronger cause,
For the power to move forward lies,
In the willingness to change and rise.

No longer bound by doubt or pain,
I face each challenge with a new refrain,
And though the road may still be long,
I know my heart is now more strong.

So here I am, a traveler transformed,
Ready to face what lies beyond,
With courage, strength, and hope in hand,
I take the next step, and the next, and the next, and...

UNUSED POTENTIAL

Be proud of who you are today,
For all your flaws and all your grace,
Embrace the person that you see,
And know that you are meant to be.

But don't forget the power within,
The potential that lies deep within,
For you have the ability to grow,
And become the best that you can show.

It's not about comparing to the rest,
But striving to be your personal best,
And reaching for the stars above,
To find the light that's filled with love.

For who you are is just the start,
Of all the greatness in your heart,
And with each step that you take,
You'll find a new path to create.

So hold on tight and don't let go,
Of all the dreams that you can sow,
For you have the potential to be,
The very best that you can see.

Be proud of who you are today,
But know that there's a brighter way,
And with each step that you can take,
You'll find the strength to stay awake.

LOST

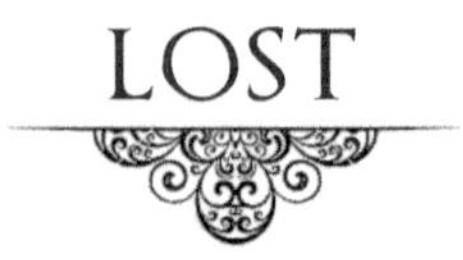

I am who they say I am,
A product of society's demand,
A puppet on a string,
A pawn in a game of branding.

I thought I knew who I was,
But now I see, it's just because,
I followed the script they wrote,
And in the process, I lost hope.

I thought I had it all,
The status, the fame, the call,
But deep inside, I felt hollow,
As if my soul had been borrowed.

I chased their dreams, their ideals,
But it was all just a guise to steal,
My identity, my true self,
And put me on a shelf.

But now I see the truth,
That I am more than just a youth,
A label, a name, a trend,
I am unique, I am a blend.

Of stories, of struggles, of pain,
Of triumphs, of love, of gain,
And though society may try,
They cannot take away what's inside.

For I am who I choose to be,
A warrior, a dreamer, a believer, me,
And though the journey may be hard,
I will always stay true to my heart.

The world around me moves so fast,
A dizzying blur that never lasts,
And in the rush, I often find,
My voice lost in the noise behind.

For everywhere I look, I see,
The pressure to be what I should be,
To follow trends and popular fads,
And forget about the dreams I had.

But in the midst of all this noise,
I hear a whisper, soft and poised,
A voice that tells me to slow down,
And focus on what truly counts.

To pay attention to my heart,
And let it guide me from the start,
To chase the dreams that light my fire,
And not just those that others desire.

For in the end, what matters most,
Is not the path that others boast,
But the journey that I choose to take,
And the memories that I create.

So I will listen to my heart,
And let it guide me from the start,
And though the road may not be clear,
I know that my path is mine to steer.

And in the end, I will stand tall,
For I followed my heart's true call,
And lived a life that was truly mine,
Full of love, purpose, and divine.

The world around me moves so fast,
A dizzying blur that never lasts,
And in the rush, I often find,
My voice lost in the noise behind.

For everywhere I look, I see,
The pressure to be what I should be,
To follow trends and popular fads,
And forget about the dreams I had.

But in the midst of all this noise,
I hear a whisper, soft and poised,
A voice that tells me to slow down,
And focus on what truly counts.

To pay attention to my heart,
And let it guide me from the start,
To chase the dreams that light my fire,
And not just those that others desire.

For in the end, what matters most,
Is not the path that others boast,
But the journey that I choose to take,
And the memories that I create.

So I will listen to my heart,
And let it guide me from the start,
And though the road may not be clear,
I know that my path is mine to steer.

And in the end, I will stand tall,
For I followed my heart's true call,
And lived a life that was truly mine,
Full of love, purpose, and divine.

Responsibility is a seed we sow,
A chance for growth, a chance to know,
What lies within our hearts and minds,
And what we're capable of when we find,

The strength to face what's on our plate,
And not just shy away or wait,
For others to take on our load,
And leave us stranded on our own.

For when we tend to our responsibility,
We open up a door to possibility,
To grow, to learn, to become more,
And leave behind what we were before.

It may not always be easy or fun,
To do what must be done,
But in the struggle, we can find,
A strength that was once left behind.

And as we tend to our responsibility,
We can discover a newfound ability,
To face life's challenges with grace,
And make the most of every day we face.

For in the end, it's not just what we do,
But how we do it, and what we pursue,
That defines the person we will be,
And the legacy we leave for eternity.

So tend to your responsibility with care,
And know that growth is always there,
Waiting for you to take the lead,
And fulfill the greatness that you need.

STARS IN THE NIGHT

In the streets, where shadows dance
And fast money seems the only chance,
Some choose to break the law for gain,
While others choose a different lane.

It's easy to get lost in the fray,
To follow the crowd and do what they say,
But there are those who choose to stand,
To hold their ground and take a different hand.

They could be out there, breaking the law,
Making quick cash and living raw,
But they choose to follow a different path,
One that's guided by a higher math.

They do the right thing, by God above,
Living with purpose and showing love,
For they know that wealth and riches fade,
But doing good will never degrade.

So when they look back on their life,
They'll know they did the right thing,
despite The temptations that came their way,
And they'll stand proud on Judgment Day.

For in the end, it's not about the cash,
But the legacy we leave that will last,
And those who choose to do what's right,
Will shine bright like stars in the night.

LOVE YOURSELF MEANS YOU LOVE ME

My love, my heart, my everything,
She's the sunshine that makes my world sing,
She loves herself, and that's a fact,
Because she knows how much I love her back.

Her confidence radiates like the sun,
And I am drawn to her like a moth to a flame,
For she takes care of what I love,
And never lets it go astray.

Her love for herself is not selfish or vain,
But rather a reflection of her inner flame,
For in loving herself, she also loves me,
And takes care of what I hold dear, you see.

She is my rock, my steady guide,
In her arms, I feel safe and warm inside,
And I know that her love for herself,
Is the reason why our love will never shelf.

So let her love herself, let her shine,
For in doing so, our love will always align,
And I will love her more each day,
For being the one who lights my way

KEEP PUSHING

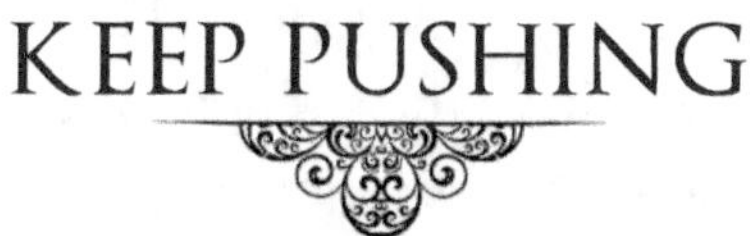

A black man in a world not right,
Where justice can be out of sight,
But he cannot give up the fight,
For he was built to succeed, and that's his right.

He faces challenges every day,
With the weight of the world on his shoulders to stay,
But he knows that giving up isn't the way,
For he was built to succeed, and that's what he'll portray.

He sees the obstacles placed in his way,
But he won't let them lead him astray,
For he knows that one day,
He'll break free from the chains of inequality's sway.

He hears the whispers behind his back,
But he knows he won't crack,
For he has the strength to attack,
And rise above the unfairness' tack.

He keeps pushing, day after day,
For he knows he'll make a way,
Through the hardships, the struggle, and the fray,
For he was built to succeed, and that's what he'll display.

So to all the black men who feel the same,
Who are fighting for their rightful claim,
Keep pushing, for you have the flame,
That will ignite the world with your name.

For you were built to succeed, to shine,
And though the road may be long and hard to climb,
Remember that you have the strength to define,
Your destiny, and make the world align.

CITY GORILLA

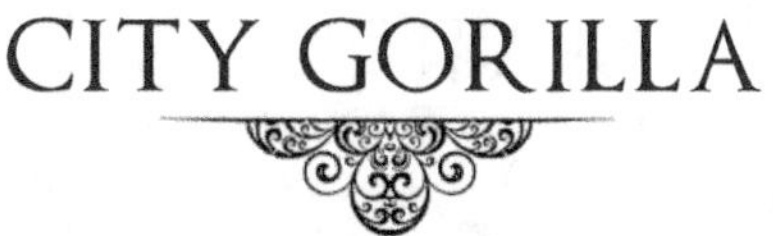

Gorillas need help, in a world they don't understand,
Their homes destroyed, their fate now in man's hand,
And in a city, filled with animals that roam,
A strong man lives, in a world not his own.

He walks the streets with a purpose and might,
A force to be reckoned with, in the wild city's fight,
But even he knows, that sometimes he needs aid,
In a world where danger can lurk in the shade.

For just like the gorillas who need help,
He too, can face challenges beyond his own self,
And though he may seem invincible and tough,
The wild city can be unforgiving and rough.

But like the gorillas, he must never give in,
For he knows that victory is born from within,
And with a heart that beats strong and true,
He'll overcome any obstacle, no matter how few.

So he fights on, with courage and grit,
And knows that sometimes, he must submit,
To the help that comes his way,
And trust in others to lead the way.

For in a world where the wild animals roam,
Strength and power can only get you so far from home,
And like the gorillas who need help to survive,
A strong man needs allies to keep his dreams alive.

THE SMART DUMMY

A smart dummy, oh what a sight,
A contradiction in its very right,
A wooden head with a brain so bright,
A genius trapped in a form so tight.

It may seem strange, a dummy with wit,
But don't be fooled, it's no counterfeit,
For its mind is sharp, and its thoughts legit,
A true marvel, you can't omit.

It's not like the others, it's quite unique,
Able to solve problems, and even critique,
With knowledge that rivals those who speak,
A smart dummy is no one to sneer or mystique.

For it proves that intelligence comes in many forms,
And that stereotypes can be the source of many norms,
It's a reminder that the mind can perform,
Even in a body that seems so lukewarm.

So let the smart dummy be a symbol of hope,
For those who feel limited by their rope,
That intelligence knows no bounds or scope,
And can be found in the most unusual of trope.

For a smart dummy is more than what it seems,
A testament to the power of dreams,
And with its brain, it can achieve great things,
A true inspiration, that leaves us in awe and gleam.